ON
SERPENT-WORSHIP
AND ON
THE VENOMOUS SNAKES
OF
INDIA

ON SERPENT-WORSHIP AND ON THE VENOMOUS SNAKES OF INDIA.

BY

SIR JOSEPH FAYRER

GYAN

Published by

GYAN

Gyan Publishing House
5, Ansari Road
Daryaganj, New Delhi-110002
Phone: 011-47034999, 9811692060
E-mail: books@gyanbooks.com

Distribution Network
gyanbooks.com
India, USA, Canada, UK, Australia

ISBN: 978-93-6433-783-0 (HB)
First Published, 1892

2nd Impression 2024

Printed at: Gyan Press, Delhi.

ON SERPENT-WORSHIP AND ON THE VENOMOUS SNAKES OF INDIA

Author: JOSEPH FAYRER

ON

SERPENT-WORSHIP

AND ON

THE VENOMOUS SNAKES

OF

INDIA.

BY

SIR JOSEPH FAYRER, K.C.S.I., LL.D., M.D., F.R.S.

BEING A PAPER READ BEFORE THE VICTORIA INSTITUTE.

PRIVATE PROOF.

ON SERPENT-WORSHIP AND ON THE VENOMOUS SNAKES OF INDIA AND THE MORTALITY CAUSED BY THEM. By Sir Joseph Fayrer, K.C.S.I., LL.D., M.D., F.R.S.

THE serpent is the ancient enemy of the human race, and it is still held in antipathy, not only by man, but by the lower animals. In man, this is probably due as much or more to the lethal properties of some forms, as to the repulsiveness of their aspect generally; while animals seem to be instinctively imbued with the dread of them. The destructive qualities, albeit the property of but few members of this large order, have come to be attributed so universally to all, that the innocent are classed with the guilty, and the harmless creature which undulates so gracefully through the grass, is popularly associated with the deadly cobra or rattlesnake.

But although dread of their baneful properties may lie at the root of the repugnance in which they are held, yet with this feeling, no doubt, has been mingled a sentiment of veneration for their supposed wisdom and supernatural power, which, combined with fear, originated one of the earliest forms of worship, in which superstition and religious feeling have found expression, for coeval with the worship of trees, the heavenly bodies, and other natural objects, we find that ophiolatry has been general throughout the world from the remotest antiquity.

Serpent-worship, according to Fergusson,* is characteristic of the Turanian races, and is rarely to be found among Aryan or Semitic peoples. There is no mention of it in the Old Testament from the formation of the Jewish nation, unless the raising of the Brazen Serpent be so considered, but six centuries later, Hezekiah "brake in pieces the brazen serpent that Moses had made; for unto those days the children of Israel did burn incense to it; and he called it Nehushtan," 2 Kings xviii, 4 and 5. Between these periods there is no other mention of it in the Old Testament, but in the book of the Wisdom of Solomon, xi, 15, we read, "They worshipped serpents void of reason"; nevertheless its revival among the Gnostic sect of the Ophites points to the fact that the notion was not extinct. "A wondrous blending of the ancient rites of Ophiolatry with mystic conceptions of Gnosticism appears in the cultus which tradition (in truth or slander) declares the semi-Christian sect of Ophites to have rendered to their tame snake, enticing it out of its chest, to coil round the sacramental bread, and worshipping it as representing the great king from heaven, who in the beginning gave to the man and woman the knowledge of the mysteries" ("Primitive Culture," Tylor).

Serpent-worship, according to Fergusson, has prevailed to a greater or less extent nearly all over the world.

In America it was known in Peru, Mexico, and among the Red Indians, according to ancient records of the United States.

Its prevalence in Western Asia seems doubtful, except in Judæa, to a slight extent in Phœnicia, and in the Troad, among the so-called Ophiogones.

As regards Europe, there are next to no traces of its prevalence among the Germans, though Tylor refers to the "Prussian serpent-worship and offering of food to the household snakes," nor among the Gauls nor Britons. Ophiolatry is said to have been practised by the Druids; according to Fergusson there is not much evidence of this, but other authorities state that the serpent's egg was the Druids' crest, and that the serpent was entwined at the foot of their altars. At Avebury in Wiltshire, there existed the figure of a serpent in stones extending for two and a half miles, of which the head and tail are still obvious. There are traces of it in

* To Fergusson's "Tree and Serpent-Worship," and Tylor's "Primitive Culture," I am indebted for much information.

Scandinavia and on the east coast of Scotland, north of the Forth, where sculptured stone monuments have been found on which the serpent appears frequently, and as a prominent figure.

In Greece the temple of Æsculapius was a centre of serpent-worship, whilst the Æsculapian rod symbolises wisdom. In this, as in other cases, the serpent was the symbol of the god, rather than itself the god.*

In Italy the serpent was often represented as the *genius loci*, but there is no direct evidence that beyond this the Romans ever worshipped it. Dante, in his "Inferno," ascribes to the serpent supernatural power, his bite causing a man to be reduced to ashes:—

> "Ed ecco ad un, ch'era da nostra proda,
> S'avventò un serpente, che'l trafisse
> Là, dove'l collo alle spalle s'annoda.
> Nè O si tosto mai, nè I si scrisse,
> Com' ei s'accese, ed arse, e cener tutto
> Convenne che cascando divenisse."
>
> (Inferno, xxiv, 97.)

It probably prevailed in Eastern Europe during the Middle Ages, and in Esthonia and Finland up to a comparatively recent period.

In Africa, Fergusson says that Sheikh Haredi in Upper Egypt is one of the best known sites of modern serpent-worship, but there are very slight traces of its prevalence in ancient Egypt. The Egyptians worshipped many animals, but there is nothing to show that the serpent was honoured above the rest.

In Abyssinia it was worshipped before the introduction of Christianity in the fourth century, and on the Guinea coast serpent-worship flourishes at the present day, and possibly has done so for the last 4,000 years.

In Eastern Asia, Persia affords but slight traces of it. The Iranians were Aryans, and brought with them fire-worship. It may have existed among their predecessors.

Cashmere was one of the principal centres of it. There is no direct testimony of its existence there till a century before the Christian era, and the latest authoritative notice of its practice was in the reign of Akbar (fourteenth century).

In Cambodia and the adjacent countries, serpent-worship reached its fullest development. The country was conquered

* For instance, when a pestilence was raging in Rome in 291 B.C., the god was brought in the form of a serpent from Epidaurus. A sanctuary was built for him on the Tiber Island.

by the Siamese in the middle of the fourteenth century, and since then it has given place, to a great extent, to Buddhism.

It prevailed also in Ceylon till the island was converted to Buddhism, in the third or perhaps the sixth century, and there are traces of it there still.

In China there are only slight traces, but the repetition of the dragon-like forms in connection with temples, pagodas, &c., in China and Burma, is suggestive of something akin to the ophidian worship.

In India it was not noticed before the Mahabhrata, but in that is mention of the Nagas, the great serpent-worshipping race, who, taking the serpent as their emblem or cognizance, came to consider themselves the descendants of serpents. There are tribes in India called Nagas at the present day.

Ophiolatry in a modified form still prevails in many parts of India. It is met with in Manipur, Cashmere, Sumbulpore, Nepaul, in many parts of the Deccan and Southern India. On the festival of Nag-Panchmee, snakes are worshipped by most of the lower tribes of the Deccan.

Serpent-worship has no place in Brahminism, but the Hindus of the present day, if they do not directly worship the snake, will neither injure nor kill, but rather propitiate it. This feeling may be as much due to fear of any bodily harm it may do them, as to the idea of its possessing supernatural powers. Tylor says the serpent has been taken as the symbol of the world, of the Tauut, or heaven-god of the Phœnicians, and as the emblem of eternity; in the latter case it is depicted with its tail in its mouth. It may have been the personification of evil in the Apophis serpent of the Egyptian Hades, and it was so in the wicked serpent of the Zoroastrians, Aji Dahaka; Ajdaha is still applied to the larger constricting snakes. Sir George Birdwood tells me that besides abstract evil, Aji Dahaka symbolised death, destruction, the storm cloud, &c. "There Ingromaniyus (Ahriman) the deadly created a mighty serpent, and snow, the work of Deva." *Cyclopædia of India* (Balfour). He also reminds me that the deadly serpent is the symbol of evil in all Eastern countries, though there, as in Greece and Rome, it may have had also a creative symbolism.

But time does not permit that I should dwell longer on this exceedingly interesting subject; I must rather describe to you those forms of the serpent in which the lethal attributes exist in their most marked conditions, producing fear and repugnance, if not the worship of olden times.

The cobra, as I have said, is an object of veneration and superstitious awe to the natives of Hindustan, for in a religion that deprecates the wrath of a cruel and relentless power which it desires to propitiate, the symbol of evil represented by this reptile is naturally regarded with peculiar deference. The rapidity and deadliness of its poison, and the large death-rate due to its bite, explain these feelings, which need cause no surprise when it is remembered that upwards of 20,000 people die yearly of snake-bite alone.

I shall give you a brief account of the most interesting forms of venomous snakes, confining myself to those that are found in our Indian Empire. It would be barely possible even to enumerate in the time at my disposal, the deadly snakes of other countries, or the innumerable innocent forms.

Wherever climate and other conditions are favourable, snakes are likely to be found, the most venomous as well as the greatest numbers in hot and tropical regions. In our own island, as well as in most parts of Europe, the common adder is the only venomous snake, and its power is feeble compared with that of the snakes of India, the West Indies, Tropical America, Africa, and Australia.

The order Ophidia is divided into Colubriform and Viperiform; the first are both venomous and innocuous, the second are all venomous. Both are numerously represented in India; the colubriform has five genera of *Elapidae*, and four of *Hydrophidae*, the viperiform has two genera of *Viperidae*, and four of *Crotalidae*, making fifteen poisonous genera, which comprise a large number of species, but this is small compared with the number of innocent colubrine snakes.

The most widely distributed venomous snakes are the viperiform; America and Africa abound in them; the *Crotalidae* are most numerous in America, the *Viperidae* in Africa, whilst poisonous colubrine snakes are most numerous in Asia.

The Ophidia are cold-blooded vertebrata, destitute of external skeleton, pectoral arch, sternum, or limbs. In a few there is a rudimentary pelvis and hinder extremities.

The body is covered by a deciduous epidermis and scales, These, with some exceptions, assume on the head and abdomen the condition of scutæ or plates. The bones of the mouth are connected by ligaments, which allow of great distension, thus enabling the creature to swallow prey larger in diameter than itself.

In snakes, one lung is much larger than the other. Their

circulation of mixed arterial and venous blood is regulated by a heart, consisting of one ventricle, and two auricles. Locomotion is effected in the terrestrial forms by the motion of the numerous ribs, which are connected indirectly with the abdominal scutæ. These act as feet, and aided by the undulations of the body, grasp the surface, thus effecting the rapid movements of which a snake is capable. The pelagic serpents swim like fish, motion being effected by the undulations of the body and of the fin-like tail.

Snakes have neither external ears nor eyelids; the eye is protected by a transparent capsule, which is shed with the epidermis. The approach of moulting is indicated by diminution in the brilliancy of the colouration, and a pearly opacity of the eye; the creature itself becoming more or less apathetic until the process is completed.

The scales and scutæ form the basis of classification. Those on the head are named as follows :—

Rostral.	Præ } Orbitals.
Anterior } Frontals.	Post } Orbitals.
Posterior } Frontals.	Upper } Labials.
Vertical.	Lower } Labials.
Supra-ciliary.	Temporals.
Occipital.	Mental.
Nasals.	Chin-shields.
Loreal.	

The form and arrangement of the scales vary. In some snakes they are plain and lie side by side, more or less lanceolate in form. In others they are imbricated, that is they overlap each other. On the head, in some snakes, they are arranged as large plates or shields. On the abdomen in the land snakes, they are in transverse plates for the purpose of locomotion. In the *Hydrophidae* and burrowing land snakes these are absent.

Snakes are oviparous and viviparous; the colubrine, except the pelagic forms, for the most part belong to the first class, the viperine to the second. The cobra lays twenty to thirty white, leathery eggs, which are hatched in some warm place by natural heat. Some are said to incubate; the python is said to coil itself round the eggs until they are hatched. The female of all snakes is said to be larger than the male; there are slight differences in colour and form, but no other external distinction.

Snakes hybernate in the cold, but returning warmth rouses them into activity. They generally eat living creatures, but some will eat eggs—the cobra robs the hen roosts, or devours insects, molluscs, and even, it is said, vegetable matter; and some are cannibals—the ophiophagus and callophis live on snakes. In captivity they will, it is said, drink milk.

Snakes differ in their habits and modes of life, and are grouped accordingly. Tree and grass snakes live in the trees, bushes, and grass, and are often coloured like the vegetation they frequent; their tails are prehensile. When slender, they are called whip snakes; innocent and poisonous forms are found among these. Ground snakes are found in all three sub-orders; the great proportion belong to this group.

Burrowing snakes live much under ground, have a rigid, cylindrical body, short tail, narrow mouth, small teeth, and are all innocent.

There are fresh-and salt-water snakes. The salt-water snakes are adapted for an aquatic life, and are venomous; the fresh-water snakes have not the same characters as the *Hydrophidae*, and are innocent—a curious fact! The *Hydrophidae* are viviparous.

I.

VIPERIFORM (*Daboia Russellii*).

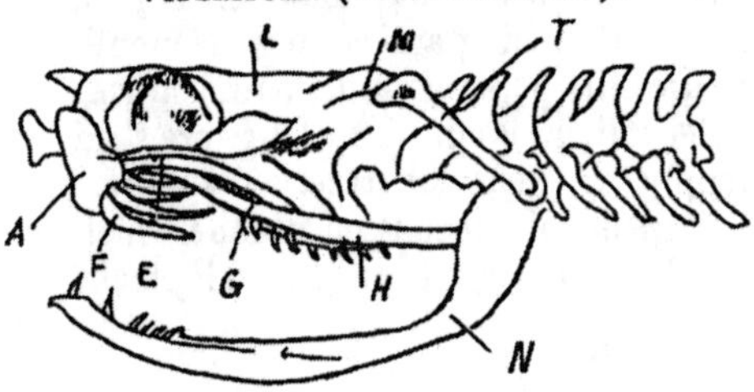

INNOCENT (*Ptyas Mucosus*).

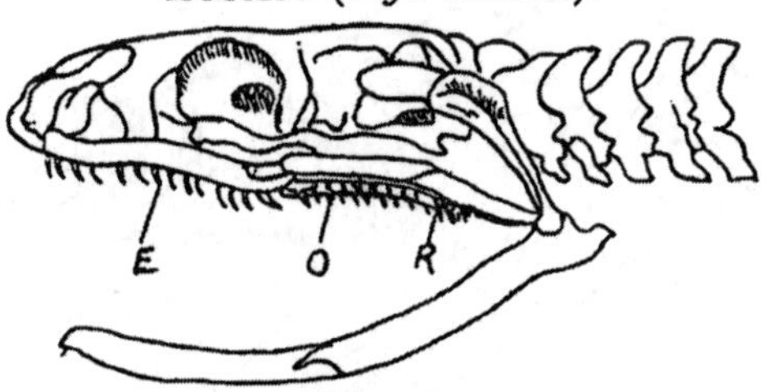

COLUBRIFORM (*Naja tripudians*).

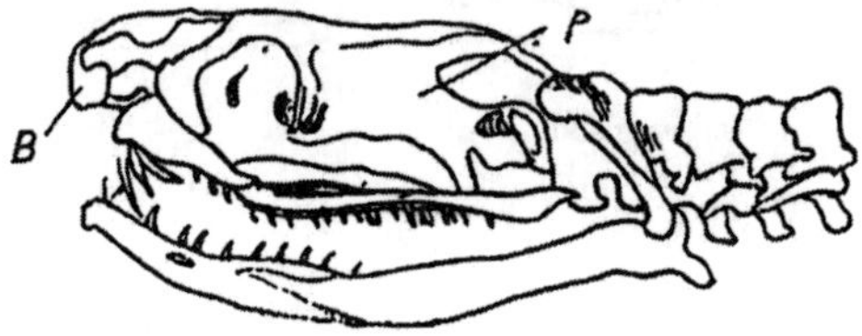

A Maxillary bone.
B Intermaxillary bone.
E Maxillary teeth.
E′ Ecto-pterygoid bone.
F Poison fang.
G Palatine bone.
H Pterygoid bone.
L Frontal bone.
M Mastoid bone.
N Mandible.
T Tympanic.
O Palatine teeth.
P Parietal bone.
R Pterygoid teeth.

Deglutition is effected in a peculiar way; the prey being seized, the mouth gapes laterally and vertically, each side of the jaws is called separately into action; the sharp and recurved teeth hold the prey firmly, as each side of the jaw alternately advances or relaxes its grasp, and it is thus gradually but inevitably engulfed.

The maxillary bones in the venomous snakes are much shorter, and provided with fewer teeth than in the innocent. In the latter, they are elongated slips of bone set with small recurved teeth. In the poisonous colubrine snakes they are less elongated and have a fixed, large poison fang several loose, reserve fangs, and one, two, or more fixed smaller teeth, not directly connected with the poison apparatus. In the *Viperidae* the maxillary bone is a short, triangular, movable wedge, furnished with a poison fang lying hidden in the mucous sheath. The movements of the fang are due to the rotation of the maxillary bone. This mobility is great in vipers, whilst it is slight in the colubrines.

When the fang is reclined or erected, the maxillary bone into which it is inserted is pushed by the external pterygoid bone, a movement which is effected by muscular action. The muscular arrangement for opening and closing the mouth at the same time compresses the poison gland, thereby injecting the venom through the tubular fang. The fangs are shed at intervals, and to supply the loss, the reserves are provided. These lie in the capsule of mucous membrane which ensheathes the fang. The fang is, during development

II.

COBRA DI CAPELLO (*Naja Tripudians*).

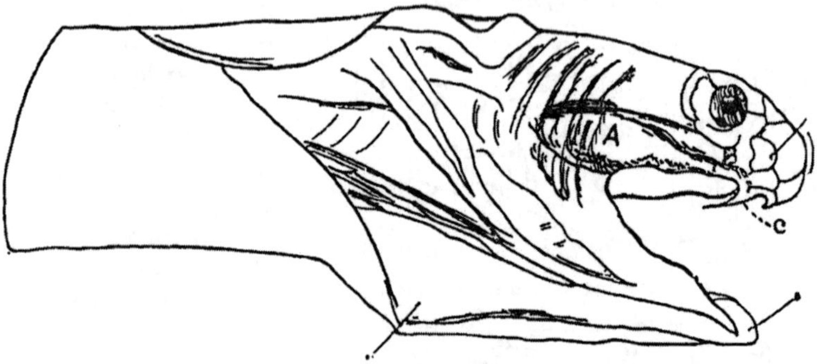

A Poison gland.
B Duct.
C Fang.

folded on itself so as to form a tube. It is along this channel that the poison passes; when the fang is deeply imbedded the quantity of virus injected is considerable, and its effects are rapidly manifested.

The poison glands are situated between the orbit and the tympanic bone; they are composed of lobes and lobules, which having secreted the virus, transmit it under muscular pressure through a duct which communicates with a triangular opening at the base of the fang. They are of various forms and sizes; in *callophis* they are much elongated; in the cobra they are of the size and something of the shape of a small almond.

The virus is a transparent, slightly viscid fluid, faintly acid in reaction, of a straw colour—in the ophiophagus, of a yellow colour; when dried it forms a semi-crystalline substance, like gum arabic. It is secreted in considerable quantities, and if a fresh, vigorous cobra be made to bite a leaf stretched across a tea-spoon—or as the natives do it, a mussel-shell, several drops may be obtained. The poison

III.

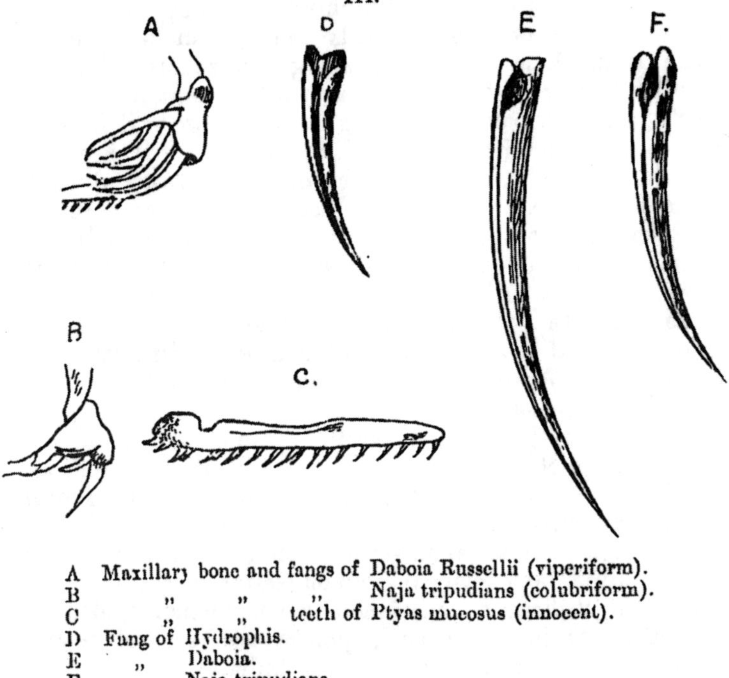

A Maxillary bone and fangs of Daboia Russellii (viperiform).
B " " " Naja tripudians (colubriform).
C " " teeth of Ptyas mucosus (innocent).
D Fang of Hydrophis.
E " Daboia.
F " Naja tripudians.

is exhausted when the snake has bitten frequently, but is rapidly reformed; in the interval the reptile is comparatively harmless, but soon becomes dangerous again. A vigorous cobra can kill several creatures before its bite becomes impotent. Removal of the fangs renders the snake temporarily harmless.

Some animals, especially the pig and the mongoose, are supposed to have immunity from snake-bite; fat sometimes protects the former, the latter is so wiry and active that it frequently escapes with only a scratch; but, if either of them be fairly bitten in a vascular part, it succumbs like any other animal.

The chemistry of snake-poison has been studied by Fontana, by Prince L. Bonaparte, Armstrong, Gautier, and others, and recently by Drs. Weir, Mitchell, and Reichert, of the United States. It is a most virulent poison, and may neither be sucked from a bite nor swallowed with impunity. It acts most rapidly on warm-blooded, but is also deadly to cold-blooded creatures, and to the lowest forms of invertebrate life. Strange to say, a snake cannot poison itself, or one of its own species, scarcely its own congeners, and only slightly any other genus of venomous snake; but it kills innocent snakes quickly. Snake-poison kills by extinguishing the source of nerve energy. It is also a blood poison and irritant, and causes great local disturbance as well as blood change. If it enter by a large vein, life may be destroyed in a few seconds. The chief effect is on the respiratory apparatus, and death occurs by asphyxia; but general paralysis is also a result. The phenomena of poisoning vary according to the nature of the snake and the individual peculiarities of the creature injured, the chief difference being observed in viperine, as contrasted with colubrine poison. The latter is a nerve-poison of great deadliness; as a blood poison its results are less marked. Viperine poison, on the other hand, is a more potent blood-poison.

Adder poison is of the viperine character, and though its immediate effects as a nerve-poison are feeble, yet those on the blood and locally on the tissues may be productive of serious symptoms.

It is impossible to enumerate all the antidotes that have been reported beneficial; but amongst those that have the greatest repute may be mentioned arsenic, ammonia, alcohol, quinine, strychnine, acids, snake poison itself, snake-bile, and the snake-stone, so much relied on in India.

These stones are said to attaeh themselves closely to the bitten part, the blood that oozes out being rapidly absorbed, and when it drops off thc bitten person is thought to be out of danger. Faraday said that these are pieees of charred bone. There may be a fragment of truth in the supposition that they are of use, because in absorbing the blood, they must also absorb some of the poison, though so little that their efficacy must bc a mere delusion.

Experiencc shows that so far no physiologieal antidote to snake-virus is known, and that, when the full effect is produeed, remedies are of little avail; but when the poison has entered in smaller quantities, medieal treatment may be of servicc.

The entry of the poison into the system should be arrested, if possible, by a ligature above the injured part; next the poison in the wound should be destroyed or removed by excision or by burning, and the application of potassium permanganate. The subsequent treatment is condueted on ordinary medical principles, of which further details would be out of place here.

I must now describe the principal venomous snakes of India. The *Elapidae* are subdivided into *Najadæ* or hooded snakes, and *Elapidae* proper, whieh are not hooded. *Najadæ* has two genera, *Naja* and *Ophiophagus; Elapidae* has three, *Bungarus*, *Xenurelaps*, *Callophis*.

Naja includes the several varieties of cobra, whieh are all of one species, though differing eonsiderably in extcrnal appearance.

The cobra di capello (*Naja tripudians*) has numerous synonyms in different parts of India. A common general native term is kala nag or kala samp. There are many varieties, and they are considcred by natives to be of different dcgrees of activity or deadliness; but the probability is that any difference is due to temporary or individual causes.

The cobras arc all hooded, bearing on the hood a spectacle mark, or a single ocellus, or no mark at all; this hood is caused by the expansion of a certain number of elongated ribs. The body and tail are rclatively of moderate length, seldom together excceding fivc or six feet, more frequently three or four fcet. The scalcs are smooth and imbricatcd; there is no lorcal shield, the nostrils are lateral and the pupil is round. The colour gcnerally is from a light chocolate, speckled, to a dark brown or even blaek. The head is short, and not very distinctly separated from the neek; the fangs are of moderate size and but slightly movable; there are one or two small teeth behind them in the maxillary bone.

Cobras are most active in the night, though often seen in the day. They will live weeks, even months in captivity, without touching food or water. They go into water readily, but are essentially terrestrial snakes. They occasionally ascend trees in search of food, and are not infrequently found in holes in walls, old ruins, fowl-houses, and among stacks of wood, cellars, old brick-kilns, old masonry of brick, or stone, or mud, among the grass or low jungle: such are the common resorts, and during the rains and inundations they collect in such places of refuge, where men, stepping on, or unintentionally disturbing them, mostly in the dark, are bitten.

The cobra sheds the epidermis with the outer layer of the cornea frequently, the fangs also are shed. The entire slough is often marked by a single rent, through which the creature has emerged, brightly coloured and glistening in its new epidermis. It aids the process of exfoliation by friction against some hard substance, such as the branches of a tree, a stone, or the like, the cast off epidermis being often found in fragments. It is oviparous, the eggs are about the size of those of a pigeon, and the shell is white, tough, and leathery.

The cobra is found all over Hindustan, up to a height of 8,000 feet. It is equally dreaded and fatal wherever met with; fortunately it is not naturally aggressive unless provoked, then raising the anterior third or more of its body, and expanding its hood, with a loud hissing it draws back its head prepared to strike, darts forward and scratches, or imbeds its fangs in the object of attack. In the latter case, the results are often dangerous and fatal, but if the fangs only inflict a scratch, or if the snake be exhausted, the same danger is not incurred. If the poison enter a large vein and be quickly carried into the circulation, death is very rapid. Men have been known to perish from a cobra bite within half an hour. The largest and strongest, as well as the smallest and weakest creatures succumb. Fortunately all who are bitten do not die. In the first place some human beings as well as lower animals have greater tolerance than others; or a wound may have been inflicted and yet but little of the poison inoculated; or in the third place, the snake may be weak or sickly, or it may have been exhausted by recent biting, and thus have become temporarily incapable of inflicting a fatal wound, though it may still poison. But when a cobra in the full possession of its power bites and injects the poison into man or beast, it is almost surely fatal, and all the vaunted antidotes are futile.

Cobras are frequently exhibited by the so-called snake charmers. Their graceful attitudes, with raised heads and distended necks, as they sway from side to side watching the movements of their keeper, and frequently striking at him, and the ease with which they are handled, make them general favourites. I may here remark that the cobra depicted in Hindoo legends or old paintings is the gokurrah, or spectacled snake. They are generally deprived of their fangs (which is done by cutting them out with a coarse knife), but the snake charmers know the habits of the creature so well that they handle them without fear, even when armed, though with great caution, always grasping them tightly below the head with one hand and holding the tail with the other. They know that a new fang is soon produced, and to prevent this they sometimes remove the capsule and reserve fangs, thus making the snake permanently harmless. The sole secret of these men lies in their dexterity and fearlessness. Their *muntras*, their antidotes, and the pipes with which they pretend to charm are as devoid of real power over the snake as are the snake-stones, roots, and other nostrums over its poison. They know that dexterity is their real security.

The snake-charmers occasionally exhibit the ophiophagus, —which, like the cobra, dilates the hood when excited—also the bungarus, daboia, and some of the innocent snakes, such as *Chrysopelia*, *Passerita*, *Ptyas*, and *Erix*, which are remarkable for the beauty of their colours, their activity, or their peculiarity of form. These exhibitions are always accompanied by the music of the pipes.

The cobra is an object of superstitious awe to the Hindus. Should fear or the death of some inmate of the house in which the cobra has taken up its abode prove stronger than superstition, it may be caught and deported in an earthen jar to some field, where it is allowed to escape, but not destroyed. Still the cobra has many enemies. Besides by its natural foes, such as the mongoose (*Herpestes*), pigs, rapacious birds, and other creatures, numbers are destroyed by low caste people for the sake of reward. But still the loss of human life is great.

The *Ophiophagus elaps* (Hamadryad, Sunkerchor) is one of the largest venomous snakes. It attains a length of ten or twelve feet, is very powerful and active, and is said to be aggressive; it is hooded like the cobra, and resembles it in general configuration. The adult is some shade of olive green or brown; the shields of the head, the scales of the neck, hinder part of the body and tail are edged with black; the body and hood are marked with black oblique bands. There are several varieties with modifications of colouration, but the general characters are essentially the same. The young differ considerably from the old, and might be mistaken for another genus; they are black, with numerous white, equidistant, narrow cross bands. The shields surrounding the occipital are large, and give a distinctive character to the adult snake. This snake, though widely distributed throughout India and in the Andaman Islands, is not common and probably does not destroy many human lives; but it is very deadly, and its virus seems to have similar effects to that of the cobra. It is found in the forest and grass jungle, and is said to live in hollow trees, and to climb them, being frequently found resting in the branches; it also takes to the water very readily. As its name implies it feeds on snakes, though probably when they are not forthcoming, it is contented with other small creatures. Its hood is smaller than the cobra's; it is even more graceful in its movements and turns more rapidly. The snake-charmers, who prize it highly, say it is very difficult to catch and handle. A fine specimen of the ophiophagus, about nine or ten feet in length, lived for some ten years in the Zoological Society's gardens, and died two or three years ago; it consumed numbers of the common English snake, and, I believe, would eat nothing else. It seemed a quiet, unaggressive creature until roused, when it would raise its head, dilate its hood, and strike at any object brought near it.

Bungarus has two Indian species. The *Bungarus cæruleus* or krait, is probably next to the cobra, the most destructive snake to human life. The other species, *B. fasciatus*, sankni, or raj-samp, is probably equally poisonous; but it is not much brought in contact with men, and therefore is less destructive to human life than *cæruleus*. The krait is of a dark, almost steel-blue black to a chocolate brown, with narrow white cross-streaks, rings, or bars of white; the ventral surface is of a dark, livid colour, or white or yellow tinge; but there are varieties in the form of colouration. This species is common all over India. The fangs are smaller than those of the cobra, and the poison is not so rapid in its action, but it is very dangerous and destructive. It is found in the fields, in grassy plains, rice fields, low, scrubby jungle, and among débris of wood and buildings. It insinuates itself into houses, into the bath-rooms, verandahs, on the ledges of doors, in book-cases and cupboards: in such situations it not infrequently causes fatal accidents. *Lycodon aulicus* is sometimes mistaken for it, but the least examination detects the difference. The scales along the dorsal region are hexagonal and very characteristic. The krait rarely attains the length of four feet.

Bungurus fasciatus, is larger than *cœruleus*, and is beautifully marked with rings of yellow on a dark steel-blue ground. The metallic lustre of the skin is very beautiful; its body is of a triangular shape, and it has hexagonal scales along the dorsal ridge. It is tolerably common in Bengal, Burmah, and Southern India, and is known in the north-west. It is found in the open country, in grass, in low jungle, and in the fields in holes in the ground, sometimes deep down among the roots of trees; it sometimes finds its way into a native hut. It feeds, like the krait, on small animals, mice, birds, frogs, lizards, probably on small snakes, and even insects. It is not very aggressive, but when attacked, retaliates fiercely. It lies coiled up, and when disturbed, jerks itself out like a spring, but does not extend its whole length of body.

Xenurelaps has only one species, which is closely allied to *Bungarus*. It is very rare, and consequently not destructive to human life.

The genus *Callophis* has several species in different parts of India, which are all more or less brilliantly coloured. They are not aggressive, and bite reluctantly, so it is sufficient to enumerate some of the species: *Callophis intestinalis, C. Macclellandi, C. anularis, C. trimaculatus, C. nigrescens, C. cerasinus*, and probably others.

The viperiform sub-order has two families, *Viperidæ*, or vipers, and *Crotalidae*, or pit-vipers. The former is represented in India by two genera, *Daboia* and *Echis*, each of which has one Indian species, viz., *Daboia Russellii* and *Echis carinata* or kuppur. *Crotalidae* has several genera; *Trimeresurus*, with seven species; *Peltopelor*, one species; *Halys*, two species; *Hypnale*, one species. These snakes are all venomous, but cause few deaths.

The *Daboia Russellii*, sometimes called cobra-monil and chain viper, is a very beautiful snake; it is of a light chocolate colour, with large, black, white-edged rings; a yellow line is on each side of the upper surface of the head, converging on the snout; rostral and labial shields yellow, with brown margin, a triangular, brown, black-edged spot behind the eye; ventral surface yellowish, or marbled with more or less numerous semi-circular brown spots, on the hinder margin of the ventral shields. It attains a considerable length, forty to fifty inches. It is common in Bengal, the south of India, Ceylon and Burmah, and probably may be found all over the plains and on the hills, up to 6,000 feet, in Cashmir, but its usual habitat is lower.

Fowls bitten by it sometimes die in less than a minute. It is nocturnal, is sluggish, and does not readily strike unless irritated, when it bites with great fury; it hisses fiercely and strikes with great vigour. Its long movable fangs are very prominent objects, and with them it is capable of inflicting deep, as well as poisoned wounds. It does not appear to cause many human deaths, but its misdeeds may be sometimes ascribed to the cobra. The daboia is said to kill cattle when grazing, by biting them about the nose or mouth. In proof of its sluggish nature, there is a well authenticated story of a young person having picked one up, and mistaking it for an innocent snake, carried it home. Its true nature was discovered when it bit a dog. It had not attempted to injure the person who carried it.

There is only one Indian species of *Echis*. *Echis carinata* (kuppur, afae). This snake is much smaller than the daboia, but grows to the length of 20 inches or more; it is terrestrial. It is found in the North-West Provinces, Punjab, Central Provinces, Scinde, and generally in the south of India, in the Anamally Hills, in the Carnatic, and in the vicinity of Madras. It is of a brownish-grey colour, with a series of quadrangular or sub-ovate whitish spots, edged with dark brown; a semi-circular band on each side of the dorsal spots enclosing a round, dark-brown, lateral spot; a pair of oblong, brown, black-edged spots on the centre of the head, converging anteriorly; a brownish spot below and a broad streak behind the eye; ventral surface, whitish, with brown specks. The scales are keeled; those on the lateral series have their tips directed downwards obliquely; the friction of these against each other causes a peculiar rustling sound.

The *Echis* is a very fierce viper; it throws itself into an attitude of defence and offence, coiled up like a spring, rustling its carinated scales as it moves one fold of the body against another. It does not wait to be attacked before darting its head and body at its enemy, the mouth wide open, and the long fangs vibrating, presenting a most menacing appearance. It is very poisonous; the virus is of the same character as that of daboia. There can be little doubt that it destroys many human lives, as men are much more exposed to contact with it than with the daboia. It is said to live largely on the *scolopendridae,* but probably it preys also on small mammals, frogs, and small birds. In some parts of India it is probably chargeable with a considerable number of deaths.

Pit vipers (*Crotalidae*) have several genera in India. They are less dangerous than their American congeners, but are all poisonous. They are remarkable for the pit or depression between the eye and nostril in the loreal region, the triangular broad head, and short, thick body.

Hypnale is the only Indian genus or species with any vestige of the caudal appendage, which has given the name of rattlesnake to certain American *Crotalidae*, and in this species it is reduced to a horny spine at the end of the tail.

Many of the Indian *Crotalidae* are arboreal snakes, and in colour resemble the foliage and branches of the trees in which they live. The Indian genera are:—*Trimeresurus; T. gramineus, T. erythrurus, T. carinatus, T. anamallensis, T. monticola, T. strigatus, T. macrosquamatus; Peltopelor; P. macrolepis; Halys, H. himalayanus, H. Elliottii; Hypnale, H. Nepa* (or carawilla). The bites of most of these do not seem to differ much in their effects from those of the English adder, except the *Hypnale nepa*, or carawilla of South India, which is more dangerous.

There remains only to notice briefly the pelagic colubrine snakes, or *Hydrophidae.* They may be recognised at once by their peculiarities. With one or two exceptions they are all venomous, and inhabit the sea, the salt-water estuaries, and the tidal streams. They have a very wide range of distribution in the Indian and Pacific Oceans. They have a great variety of form, but the transitions are very gradual; some attain a considerable length; I have not seen one of more than five feet, but no doubt they often exceed this. They are very poisonous, and though accidents are rare, yet fatal cases are on record. The fishermen and sailors on the coasts know their dangerous properties, and avoid them.

The *Hydrophidae* have smaller heads, jaws and fangs than the land snakes; the fangs have open grooves in some, but not all. The virus is very active, and appears to operate as speedily and certainly as that of the land snakes. They have an elongated body like the latter; in some instances it is short and thick; in others it is very thick towards the tail, and most disproportionately elongated and attenuated in the neck, whilst the head is very minute. The colouration is varied, often brilliant and beautiful. The hinder part of the body and tail is flattened and compressed vertically, almost like the fin or tail of a fish, and they swim with ease and rapidity. When thrown on the land by the surf, as they frequently are, they are helpless. Their food is fish and small aquatic creatures. There are certain parts of the Bay of Bengal where they may be seen in great numbers, and their movements in the blue water are agile and beautiful. There are four genera in the Indian seas; *Platurus*, *Enhydrina*, *Pelamis*, *Hydrophis*. *Platurus* has two species, *P. scutatus* and *P. Fischeri* (Bay of Bengal, tidal streams near Calcutta). This genus has several characters of the land snakes, *e.g.*, well-marked ventral shields; body sub-cylindrical, and not compressed like *Hydrophis;* the colour is black, tinged with yellow.

Enhydrina has only one species, *Enhydrina bengalensis* (valakadyen); it is very poisonous; body and tail compressed, belly carinate; colour, bluish-grey, with dark bands of same, though deeper colour; no ventral shields. *Pelamis* has only one species, *P. bicolor*. This is one of the most remarkable sea-snakes in the Bay of Bengal; no ventral shields, body flattened, yellow sides and belly, back black; it is called kullundur, and is very poisonous.

Of *Hydrophis* the species are numerous; in the Indian seas about thirty have been described, and there are probably others. They present a considerable variety of form and colouration; some have elongated necks and small heads, the posterior part of the body being larger than the anterior: others have not this characteristic, but they all have a strong family likeness, and may be recognised at once by their compressed bodies, fin-like tails, and the general absence of well marked ventral scutæ. Their colouring is also remarkable, green, yellow, black, in bands or rings being a common pattern. They are pelagic, though they enter the tidal rivers; they seldom live long in captivity.

The mortality from snake-bite in India is very great. The average loss of life during the eight years ending 1887 has been 19,880 human beings, and 2,100 head of cattle yearly. Mr. V. Richards said the cobra causes nine-tenths of the human deaths. The snakes which are most destructive to life are so probably in the following order:—the cobra,

Naga tripudians; the krait, *Bungarus cæruleus;* the kupper. *Echis carinata*; Russell's viper, *Daboia Russellii;* the hamadryas, *Ophiophagus elaps;* the raj-samp, *Bungarus fasciatus.*

Deaths from Snake-Bite in India in 1889 and 1890.

In Madras in 1889, 1,587 human beings, and 2,037 cattle were killed; 340 snakes were destroyed at a cost of Rs. 49. In 1890, 1,424 human beings, and 1,852 cattle were killed; no snakes were destroyed.

In Bombay in 1889, 1,080 human beings, and 74 cattle were killed; 433,795 snakes were destroyed at a cost of Rs. 7,848. In 1890, 1,075 human beings, and 100 cattle were killed; 406,092 snakes were destroyed at a cost of Rs. 7,136.

In Bengal in 1889, 10,681 human beings, and 480 cattle were killed; 41,189 snakes were destroyed at a cost of Rs. 3,439. In 1890, 10,534 human beings, and 538 cattle were killed; 41,115 snakes were destroyed at a cost of Rs. 3,742,

In the North-West Provinces and Oudh, in 1889, 6,445 human beings, and 221 cattle were killed; 25,663 snakes were destroyed at a cost of Rs. 3,137. In 1890, 5,798 human beings, and 247 cattle were killed; 24,083 snakes were destroyed at a cost of Rs. 2,902.

In the Punjab, in 1889, 915 human beings, and 87 cattle were killed; 68,501 snakes were destroyed at a cost of Rs. 8,232. In 1890, 834 human beings, and 32 cattle were killed; 29,941 snakes were destroyed at a cost of Rs. 4,313.

In the Central Provinces in 1889, 1,063 human beings, and 14 cattle were killed; 1,395 snakes were destroyed at a cost of Rs. 558. In 1890, 1,041 human beings, and 54 cattle were killed; 1,554 snakes were destroyed at a cost of Rs. 565.

In Lower Burma in 1889, 208 human beings, and 689 cattle were killed; 6,178 snakes were destroyed, but no rewards given. In 1890, 223 human beings, and 731 cattle were killed; 6,319 snakes were destroyed, but no rewards given.

In Assam, in 1889, 230 human beings, and 71 cattle were killed; 395 snakes were destroyed at a cost of Rs. 23. In 1890, 214 human beings, and 257 cattle were killed; 478 snakes were destroyed at a cost of Rs. 14.

In Coorg in 1889, 1 person was killed; 14 snakes were

destroyed at a cost of Rs. 3. In 1890, 2 cattle were killed; 26 snakes were destroyed at a cost of Rs. 6.

In the Hyderabad Assigned Districts in 1889, 216 human beings, and 120 cattle were killed; 76 snakes were destroyed at a cost of Rs. 26. In 1890, 191 human beings, and 132 cattle were killed; 113 snakes were destroyed at a cost of Rs. 29.

In Ajmere and Merwara in 1889, 53 human beings were killed; 224 snakes were destroyed at a cost of Rs. 10. In 1890, 78 human beings and 3 cattle were killed; 192 snakes were destroyed at a cost of Rs. 20.

In Bangalore, in 1889, 1 human being was killed; 645 snakes were destroyed at a cost of Rs. 231. In 1890, no human beings nor cattle were killed; 746 snakes were destroyed at a cost of Rs. 277.

Throughout India, in 1889 there were 22,480 human beings and 3,793 cattle killed by snakes, while 578,415 snakes were destroyed at a cost of Rs. 23,556. In 1890, there were 21,412 human beings and 3,948 cattle killed; while 510,659 snakes were destroyed at a cost of Rs. 19,004.

"The average result for all the Provinces, shows a mortality of one to every 10,155 of population in 1890, as compared with one to every 9,673 in 1889. The Provinces which showed the greatest loss of life from snake-bite in proportion of population (excluding Ajmere and Merwara) are Bengal (1 to 6,731), the North-West Provinces and Oudh (1 to 8,094), and the Central Provinces (1 to 10,350). The lowest mortality (about 1 to 25,000 of population) occurred in Madras, the Punjab, and Assam."—*Report of Indian Government*, 1891.

As regards the measures to be adopted for reducing the annual loss of life by snake-bite, the chief points are to make known the appearance and habits of the poisonous snakes, and to institute proper rewards for their destruction. With a plain description, and a faithful representation in colour of each species, such as the Government of India have been put in possession of, the people can easily be made acquainted with the characters that distinguish the venomous from the harmless snakes, and thus learn to avoid or to destroy them.

Until some measures are more uniformly resorted to, there will be no material diminution in the loss of human life from snake-bite, which cannot now be rated at less than 20,000 annually.

It is satisfactory to find that the Government of India are insisting upon the institution of measures having for their object the destruction of snakes. It is, however, to be feared that the last measure proposed, *i.e.*, the cutting down and clearing away of jungle in the vicinity of villages, can hardly be expected to have the desired effect, for the reason that the poisonous snakes do not frequent the sort of jungles that surround villages so much as they do other localities, such as ruins, holes in walls and in the ground, grass and cultivated fields, &c., and that also the probability is that a great proportion of bites are inflicted far from the villages, where such clearances as those proposed by Government could not be effected, even were they useful. I would suggest that a reward should be given for each poisonous snake and for no other; there can be no difficulty in identifying them. This could only be effected by an organised system carried out generally in every district in which poisonous snakes exist. If it were decided to try this plan as universally as it is proposed to cut down the jungle, it is probable that a diminution of the evil might be expected; but whatever efforts are made they should be universally sustained and continuous. It is quite admitted that the problem is a difficult one to solve, but no effort should be spared to mitigate what must be regarded as a preventible cause of death.